Make 22 Herbal Gifts for the Holidays

Compiled by Rachael Kelly

The mission of Storey Communications is to serve our customers by publishing practical information that encourages personal independence in harmony with the environment.

Padded Hangers with Moth Repelling Potpourri

Padded hangers are one of those special little gifts that are always appreciated. Use a wooden coat hanger without a pants bar. Measure the wooden part from the center to one end — you will make the cover in halves. Make a satin tube 1 inch longer than half the length of the hanger and about 1½ inches wide. (You can double 1½-inch-wide satin ribbon and stitch along each selvage.) Stitch across one end of the tube and leave the other end open. Turn the stitched tube right side out, and slip over one end of the hanger. Repeat for the other end. Fill each side tightly with potpourri, and blind stitch the ends together at the center. Wrap the hook with narrow ribbon, holding it in place over the end with white glue. Wrap the other end once around the hanger to hide the seam, and stitch it in place. Cover the end with a bow tied around the handle.

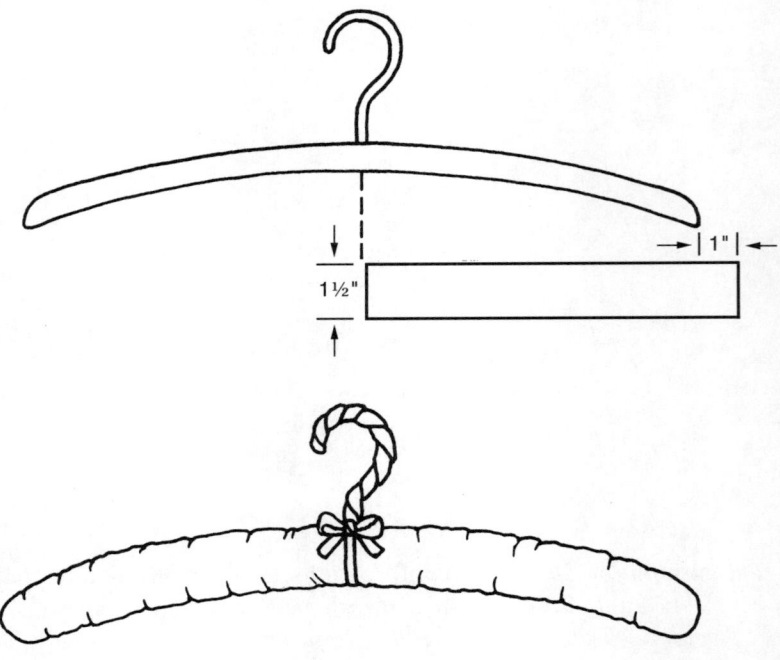

HERBITAGE FARM'S MOTH POTPOURRI

For the oils mentioned you can use either fragrance or essential oils, which can be obtained at craft stores, natural food stores and through some mail-order catalogues.

- ½ cup cedar shavings
- ¼ cup pennyroyal
- ¼ cup lavender
- ¼ cup santolina or southernwood
- ¼ cup peppermint
- ¼ cup lemon verbena
- ¼ cup thyme
- ¼ cup rosemary
- ¼ cup orrisroot
- ⅛ cup whole cloves
- ⅛ cup lemon peel
- ⅛ cup black peppercorns
- 6 drops cedar oil
- 6 drops lemon oil
- 6 drops lavender oil

This project/recipe by Barbara Radcliffe Rogers appeared in *Herbal Treasures*.

Spice-Filled Trivets and Mug Mats

These trivets and mug mats do double duty: they protect tables and counters from your hot mug or casserole and release a fragrant scent at the same time.

Several weeks before you put your trivet or mat together, make the spice and oil mixtures. Using the ingredients listed, combine oils and spices, and let sit, covered, for 3 weeks.

To make a 9-inch x 9-inch trivet, use the following directions; to make a 4-inch x 4-inch mug mat use measurements in parentheses.

The pattern features a lap seam so that the spice pouch can be easily removed when the cases need laundering. The recipe for spice oil makes 60 drops, or 1 dram of oil — enough to scent 1 pound of spices. If you wish to stencil, silk-screen, or embroider a design on your trivet or mat, plan the design to fit a 6-inch (3-inch) square centered top to bottom and end to end.

To make the case you will need one piece of fabric 10 inches by 24 inches (5 inches by 13 inches). You will also need a piece of fabric 7 inches by 13 inches (3½ inches by 7 inches) for the spice pouch.

1. On short ends of case fabric piece, fold over ½ inch (½ inch) twice, and press. No need to sew, as topstitching in Step 3 will hold folds in place.
2. Fold piece into thirds, with end folds facing out and with the left-hand end overlapping the right-hand end by the width of the folds. The overlap should occur at the center of the piece. Press flat.
3. Sew ½ inch (¼ inch) seams along the sides. Trim corners, turn inside out, and press. Topstitch 1½ inches from the edge (½ inch) all the way around.
4. To make spice pouch, make ½ inch (½ inch) folds in each short end of the fabric piece, and press. Fold the entire piece in half at the center, with the end folds facing out. Press.
5. Stitch long edges in ½ inch (¼ inch) seams, leaving short end open. Trim corners and turn inside out.
6. Insert up to 1 cup (¼ cup) of the spice mixture into the inside pouch. Whipstitch or machine stitch closed. Tuck pouch into case.

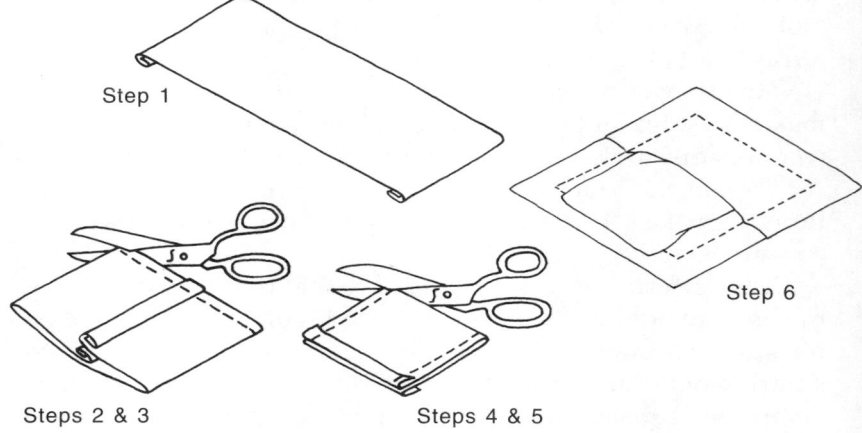

Step 1

Steps 2 & 3

Steps 4 & 5

Step 6

SPICE MIXTURE
YIELD: 1 POUND

4 ounces cinnamon pieces, ¼ inch or smaller
3 ounces whole allspice
2 ounces orange peel, potpourri-cut or smaller
1 ounce whole cloves
1 ounce rosemary leaves
1 ounce star anise, broken into pieces
1 ounce oakmoss, cut and sifted
½ ounce crushed nutmeg
½ ounce ginger, cut and sifted

Spice Oil
YIELD: ENOUGH TO SCENT 1 POUND OF SPICES

14 drops each of cinnamon, allspice, and sweet orange (or bergamot) oils
10 drops clove oil
8 drops nutmeg oil

This project/recipe by Sally Booth-Brezina appeared in *Herbal Treasures*.

Scented Stationery

Purchase a box of stationery. Cut a piece of blotter paper and a piece of shirt cardboard to fit your stationery box. Drop a few drops of your favorite essential oils onto the blotter paper and place it on the shirt cardboard. Cover the blotter paper with a couple of layers of cheesecloth, then with a print fabric. Glue the fabric edges around to the back of the cardboard. Put this in the bottom of the box and replace the stationery. The layers of cloth prevent the writing paper from becoming spotted with oil. This makes a nice gift.

This project by Bob Clark appeared in *Herbal Treasures*.

Homemade Cosmetic Gifts

Creams and scrubs you make and bottle specially, maybe with a satin bow, are a treat. Minty Astringent can be used as a men's aftershave too.

ALL-PURPOSE SCRUB

½ cup ground oatmeal
⅓ cup ground sunflower seeds
4 tablespoons almond meal
½ teaspoon ground peppermint, spearmint, or rosemary leaves
dash cinnamon powder
water, milk, or heavy cream

Mix dry ingredients together thoroughly. Use approximately 2 teaspoons of scrub mixture for the face, more for the body, and enough water (for oily skin), milk (for normal skin), or heavy cream (for dry skin) to form a spreadable paste. Use blender or food processor to mix.

Allow to thicken for 1 minute. Massage onto face and throat or body area. Rinse. Prep time about 10 minutes.

This scrub is good for all skin types, and can be used daily. Follow with a moisturizer. Store in a zip-seal bag, low tub/jar, or a tin. Leaves skin very smooth.

YIELDS: 4 TO 24 TREATMENTS, DEPENDING ON USE.

MINTY ASTRINGENT

1 tablespoon fresh peppermint, spearmint, or lemon balm (if dried, use 1½ teaspoons of the herb)
1 cup witch hazel

Combine the ingredients in a jar with a tight-fitting lid. Allow herb to steep for 1 week. Strain. Use 1 teaspoon per application. Refrigeration not required. Shake jar occasionally during the week. Store in a bottle or spritzer.

This recipe is good for those with normal and oily skin and can be used daily. Follow with a moisturizer.

ABOUT 48 TREATMENTS.

Recipes appeared in *The Herbal Body Book*, by Stephanie Tourles.

Tiny Tussies for the Tree

Miniature tussie mussies make elegant Christmas ornaments and are easily made from tiny, dried rosebuds, little sprigs of baby's breath, pieces of statice, and other dried flowers. This is a perfect way to use the pieces that have broken off in the process of making herbal wreaths (see page 9).

Cut a piece of sheet Styrofoam (well-washed meat trays work perfectly) about the size of a nickel. Push a 4-inch length of doubled florist's wire through it to make a handle in the center. Push the stems of the herbs into the Styrofoam, using a single little rosebud in the center and other rosebuds or tiny sprigs around it.

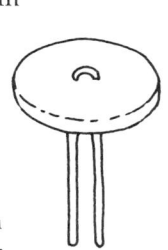

Use single florets of statice, tansy, and others to make a tiny bouquet, and then fill in the spaces with little whole cloves, tiny sprigs of baby's breath, leaves of boxwood, or other tiny blossoms. Glue these in place with tacky glue.

When the bouquet is dry, you can glue around the edge a small piece of narrow, gathered lace or little ruffles, cut from paper doilies. Cover the back with a circle of white Styrofoam. Wrap the florist's wire stem with florist's tape, and finish off with a tiny bow of ¼-inch wide, satin picot ribbon, in a complementary or matching color. Add a loop of nylon thread for a hanger.

If you don't have rosebuds, you can use a very small strawflower for your center or you can simply group your other flowers. If the flowers have stems ½ inch or longer, you can bundle your blossoms into a bouquet, tie with heavy thread, and wrap with florist's tape. To the base of the stem, glue a ruffle of slightly wider lace or eyelet gathered into a circle. Although full-sized tussie mussies can be used on the tree, these miniature ones are so delicate and dainty that they are certain to steal the show.

This project by Barbara Radcliffe Rogers appeared in *Herbal Treasures*.

Miniature Lace Wreaths

Form a 1½–2-inch diameter circle using white florist wire. For ease, form the circle around a bottle or other round object of the desired size. Do not fasten the wire ends, but allow them to overlap about 1 inch.

Using one end of the wire as though it were a needle (you may have to smooth "the needle" slightly with steel wool), thread ½–¾-inch wide ecru or white lace onto the circle. Use about ½ yard of lace, or enough to form a full, gathered circle. Loop the ends of the wire together, and trim off excess. If the lace is not fairly stiff, give the wreath a quick spray of starch and allow it to dry thoroughly. Decorate by gluing on tiny dried herb blossoms, such as individual chive blossom florets, little clusters of marjoram flowers, tansy or costmary buttons, feverfew, leaves of thyme, germander, boxwood, and seeds or berries such as bay and coriander. Finish by attaching a loop for hanging and a bow of ⅛-inch satin ribbon in a complementary color.

This project by Barbara Radcliffe Rogers appeared in *Herbal Treasures.*

Queen Anne's Lace Snowflakes

This takes a little forethought, but it's well worth the effort and sure to become a tradition. In the summer, while Queen Anne's lace flowers are in full bloom, gather a number of blooms of different sizes. Snip the stems leaving just enough to hold it together. Press the flowers open flat between sheets of paper and put a weight on top. A flower press works well. Leave for several weeks until dry.

Shortly before you want to use them, give the snowflakes a spritz of hairspray to help them hold up. Tuck them into the branches of your tree. If you think they may slip, a touch of glue from a glue gun will hold them in place.

Crafting an Herbal Wreath

When your herb gardens are bulging with large vigorous plants, it's time to begin selecting the tussie bundles for your herbal wreath. Variety is the key to creating an exciting herbal wreath. For variety in color, collect a number of different greens, from the bright hue of Italian parsley to the dark emerald greens of the mints. For variety in texture, the soft woolly lamb's ears and pebble-patterned sage are good examples. Sharp accents add sparks and excitement. Silvery artemesias combined with opal basil make an excellent eye-pleaser.

Another important consideration is scent. Adding scented geraniums, cinnamon and licorice basils, sweet Annie, and scented southernwoods to wreaths contributes to the overall texture and color, as well as adding fragrance. Wreaths can also be scented with essential oils.

To prepare herbs for drying, gather them in bundles of five to seven stems, each about 4 or 5 inches long. Wrap each bundle together with a rubber band, and fasten it over a wire coat hanger as shown.

Add wrapped herb bundles to the hanger until it is full, and then hang in an airy, dark place to dry. Do not overcrowd the herbs on the hanger or they will dry unevenly, or possibly mildew. Nine herb bundles per hanger dry well. An 18-inch diameter wreath — very full and lush, with no skimping — will require about five or six hangers full of herbs.

The herb bundles, when thoroughly dry and papery to touch, are attached to a straw base with fern pins. The day before you plan to make the wreath, insert a fern pin, with the notch facing upward, into a spot on the back of a wreath form that has been slathered with tacky glue, see drawing. About ¾ inch of the pin should be left exposed for ease in hanging. Let the glue dry thoroughly before beginning the wreath.

This hanger is sufficiently strong to hold any herb- or flower-based wreath up to 24 inches in diameter. Larger wreaths, or those employing heavier materials, will require a wire hanger looped and twisted around the straw wreath base.

To begin, lay the straw base on newspaper (you can save for your next potpourri any loose herbs that crumble off as you work) and take all the dried herb bundles off the hangers. Remove the rubber bands; once dried, each herb bundle should remain intact. Take note of all the different colors, textures, and sparks, or accents, you have available, and begin to formulate a design in your mind.

There are two basic rules to wreathmaking. First, work the herb material in a random fashion around the wreath, contrasting the colors, textures, and accents by placing smooth leaves next to fuzzy ones, bright greens next to silvers, and so on. Second, place all of the herb bundles in the same direction, generously overlapping the herbs. This method covers the fern pins and gives fluidity and consistency to the final form.

Working within these parameters, begin in the center, or face, of the ring by using fern pins to fasten the herb bundles in place. This is in reverse of the technique required for constructing other types of wreaths. Herb bundles are fragile so it is important to work in this order, otherwise the herbs may be crushed. Continue adding bundles to the outside of the ring, and then to the inside of the ring. Keep the wreath lush and full.

If you wish to add a focal point to your wreath, attach a flourish of comfrey leaves clustered with Chinese lanterns and sprigs of sweet Annie. The comfrey leaves eventually turn a lovely bronze. Any cluster of color or unusual dried materials can provide a focal point wherever you wish it on the wreath.

When the wreath is completed, hang it, and fill in any spots you may have missed, working carefully with the dried materials at this point. When the wreath is hung, gravity tends to pull materials down on the left side and at the bottom, making these trouble spots on many wreaths. There are two remedies. You can hold materials up with small dabs of tacky glue, used very sparingly, in strategic spots. Or, you can pin through the edge of the stray plant material, pushing the pin in only to the point where the herb should be positioned. Cover the pin by pulling some of the neighboring herb over it to conceal it.

Occasionally, you may wish to neaten the final wreath by snipping away any small, stray herb sprig. Try not to overdo this, or your wreath will look unnatural. Hang the wreath away from bright light and it will give you years of pleasure.

WREATHMAKING BOTANICALS

Artemesia
Basil
Bergamot
Boxwood
Burnet
Catnip
Comfrey
Coriander
Costmary
Curry plant
Fennel
Germander
Horehound
Hyssop
Lamb's ears
Lavender
Lemon balm
Lemon verbena
Lovage
Marjoram
Mint
Oregano
Patchouli
Rosemary
Sage
Santolina
Scented geraniums
Sweet woodruff
Tansy
Thyme
Winter savory
Yarrow

This project by Linda Fry Kenzle appeared in *Herbal Treasures*.

Live Herbal Wreaths

Living herbal wreaths are a wonderful way to use grown herbs after the weather becomes too severe to enjoy them outdoors. Live wreaths, which are not difficult to make, can be stunning centerpieces or can be used as a surrounding decoration for a punch bowl, fruit bowl, or candle.

I decide the size of my living wreaths according to the plates I have available. Large, round trays work well for bigger wreaths; saucers make good containers for wreaths intended to surround candles.

A box-wreath frame (the double-wire type made in two layers) slightly smaller than your plate is ideal, but not absolutely necessary. Fill the box frame with sphagnum moss, or wrap pieces of sphagnum around a single-wire frame, and tie the moss loosely with heavy thread to hold it in place. For a candle wreath, you can use a macramé ring or a plastic coffee-can lid with the center cut away. The ring base will be completely covered, so it doesn't matter what it looks like. Whatever you use, don't pack the sphagnum too tightly.

Gather herbs, especially those with soft stems that propagate by layering, such as creeping thyme. This excellent base can be supplemented with stems of rosemary, boxwood, germander, lavender, mint, marjoram, savory, and sage. Begin

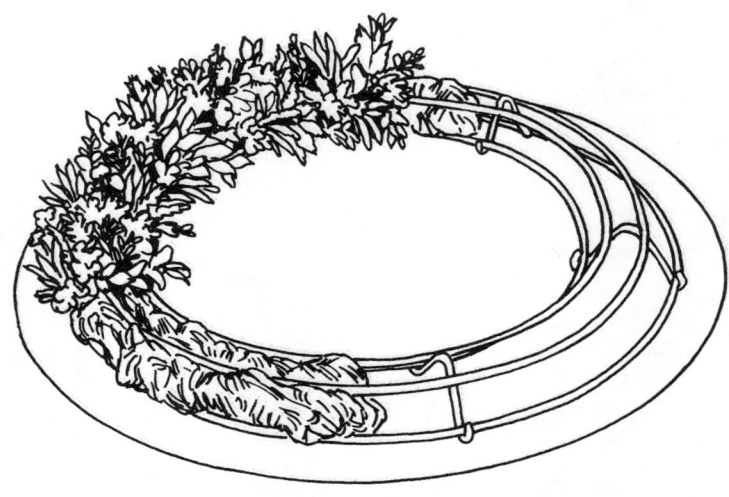

with the thyme, or whatever soft-stemmed herb you have. Try to have some roots on the plants, if possible. Press the roots or the stems into the moss as firmly as possible, winding the herb stems into the shape of the wreath. How you do this will depend on the herbs you have, their length, and how easily they bend. Save those herbs with larger leaves for last and use them as accents.

If you are making your wreath at a time of year when you have small plants, you can tuck their roots, with a small ball of potting soil still attached, into the sphagnum. Basil, chamomile, and even violets or small salad burnet plants may be used; small-rooted scented geraniums work well. These plants, and those cuttings which form roots, will continue to live in the moist sphagnum.

When your wreath is the way you like it, fill the base plate or tray with water and set the wreath in it. After a few hours, check it. The point is for the moss to absorb plenty of water, but once it has become thoroughly wet, pour off any excess water in the dish. You don't want your wreath to become waterlogged.

Live wreaths made in mid- to late-October will be lush for the holidays. I suggest keeping the freshly made wreath out of direct light for the first few days, especially if you want the cuttings to take root. A rooting hormone and frequent mistings are beneficial.

Gradually move the wreath under more light, either a sunny window or indoor lights; apply weak feeding of fertilizer when watering. These procedures will definitely prolong the life of the wreath, as the sphagnum moss is a sterile soil and any rooted plants will have the same nutrient requirements inside as they do outside.

For special occasions, push fresh flowers with a few inches of stem into the moss. They will keep as they would in a vase. Over a period of time, some things in your wreath will grow and need to be pruned or woven back into the wreath; others will wilt and need to be replaced. A living wreath, like a living garden, requires some care, but brings much pleasure indoors when there's little greenery outdoors!

This project by Barbara Radcliffe Rogers appeared in *Herbal Treasures*.

A Spice Wreath

The perfect accent for the kitchen, this wreath is a fragrant, attractive decoration, as well as a conversation piece. The Creative Twist paper ribbon loops give the wreath a nice, plump, airy aspect. The materials list includes enough supplies to make six wreaths.

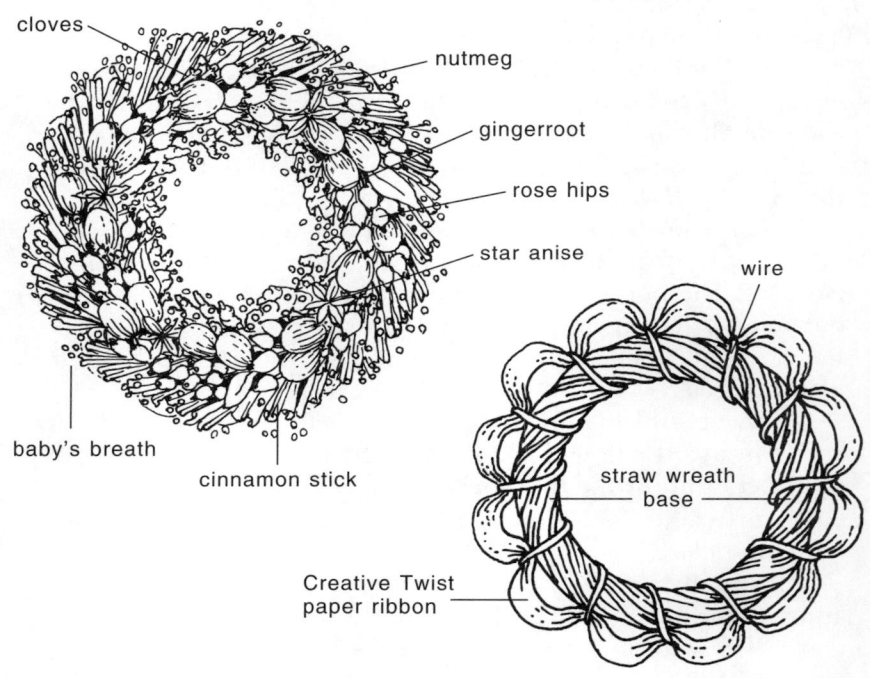

Supplies

Six 6-inch straw wreath bases
Six 48-inch lengths Creative Twist paper ribbon, in colors of your choice
Fine wire (or nylon thread in several thicknesses)
Hot glue
1 bunch baby's breath
8 ounces whole nutmeg
8 ounces 3-inch cinnamon sticks
8 ounces gingerroot
8 ounces star anise
4 ounces rose hips, whole
4 ounces whole cloves
4 ounces whole allspice

Directions

1. Unravel the Creative Twist ribbon.
2. Attach the end of a 48-inch (approximately) piece of wire securely around a starting point on the wreath base.
3. Fasten the Creative Twist paper to the outside of the wreath with the wire, wrapping the wire around the wreath at about 1-inch intervals, and pulling up the paper to make 1-inch loops. The wreath will be encircled by about twelve paper loops when you are done. Bind off the end of the wire securely.
4. With wire, make a hanging device at the top back of the wreath.
5. Hot-glue the cinnamon sticks all around the surface of the wreath in a slanted fashion going in one direction. Fill in any spaces with cinnamon sticks that have been cracked in half cross-wise (use a hammer to crack the sticks).
6. Hot-glue the gingerroot pieces to the inner surface of the wreath.
7. Use hot glue to attach the nutmeg, star anise, clusters of cloves and allspice, and groupings of three rose hips. Space these spices in attractive clusters on top of the cinnamon sticks.
8. Pinch off 1½–inch long clusters of baby's breath, and hot-glue them in between the Creative Twist paper loops on the outer edge of the wreath. Glue more clusters of baby's breath to the surface of the wreath, sparingly, to fill gaps.
9. The wreath may be sprayed with hair spray to help preserve it, or you may prefer to brush cinnamon oil on the cinnamon sticks and other spices to enhance and preserve the fragrance.

This project by Grace M. Wakefield appeared in *Herbal Treasures*.

Herb Pillows

There is no luxury quite akin to laying a tired head upon a pillow filled with herbs and fragrant flowers. The scent of a spring garden or of the woods on a summer afternoon is sure to conjure up dreams of happy times. While any pillow feels better if it carries a pleasant fragrance, certain herbs comfort in special ways.

Hops, for example, have been known for centuries to help induce a normal, natural sleep. We now know that it is because of the lupulin they contain. The kings of England are said to have slept on pillows of hops when the headaches of state robbed them of sleep.

Dill is known to have a calming effect on cranky babies, and its very name is thought to come from a word meaning "to lull." Lavender will soothe a headache, although its invigorating scent does not promote sleep.

As pillow stuffing, however, herbs are way behind feathers! We must find a way, therefore, to put the potpourri in the pillow without filling it with rustling, often bumpy and bristly leaves and flowers.

The herb pillow doesn't replace the big bed pillow—it supplements it. They are small, flat packets, like large sachets, lace-edged and stitched of quilted fabric to pad against sharp little stems. They can be as small as 6 inches square or up to 8 by 10 inches. The lace can be any soft variety, narrow for the smaller pillows and wider for the larger sizes. The fabric is always a pastel, usually soft, elegant floral. Look for remnants of chintz or other cotton decorator fabrics, and line them with a layer of quilt batting sandwiched between the outer fabric and muslin lining.

Use plenty of potpourri, but don't fill it so it bulges; it should be fairly flat. Unfortunately, hops are not sweet-smelling; they have an almost acrid odor, like a campfire of poplarwood. Hops should be mixed with at least equal parts of a potpourri strong enough to let it blend in. Since strong, invigorating herbs like mint and lavender cannot be used, lemon verbena saves the night, with its fresh, lemon scent that lasts forever.

Mix lemon verbena, rose petals (removing the lumpy buds to be used in blends where they'll be seen and not felt), chamomile, rosemary, and a little rose oil and very little chipped orrisroot. Because of its possibly irritating nature and the allergic reactions some folks experience, orrisroot should be used sparingly, if at all, and never in powdered form in herb pillows. Equal parts of this potpourri and hops create a pleasant, fragrant blend for pillows.

Less fancy, but equally effective, are flat, muslin packets of this potpourri which can be placed inside the pillow cover. It is best to tack them to the center with a stitch or two so the packets won't slip about.

A dill pillow for the baby should be a very flat little packet of dillweed. If you use lace, be sure it is narrow and quite soft. Avoid ribbons or bows on pillows meant for babies and adults alike.

Botanic print fabrics with framed designs (available at fabric stores) make perfect herb pillows. Choose a backing fabric to match either the border frame or the main color in the flowers. Use a matching, corded piping along the edge. Just before stitching the pillow closed, tuck a packet of pink rose petals right behind the print.

You needn't be limited to florals. These squares are available with Christmas scenes (which would be nice filled with balsam), with seashells (a perfect setting for a seashore potpourri of bay, thyme, rosemary, balsam, and beach roses), or with wild bird or duck prints (suitable for a man's study, filled with a packet of cedar shavings, balsam, lemon verbena, oakmoss, and whole cloves).

This project by Barbara Radcliffe Rogers appeared in *Herbal Treasures*.

Fragrant Decorative Yule Log

This looks wonderful in front of the fireplace or on top of a woodstove.

> Oakmoss, or other moss
> Small log (real or artificial)
> White glues, such as Tacky or Velveret
> Frankincense and myrrh potpourri, see recipe
> Two 10-inch cinnamon sticks
> Star anise
> Whole cloves
> Pine cones in various sizes
> Fragrant oils, such as cinnamon, clove, or frankincense
> Red or green satin bow
> Feathered dove or cardinal, optional
> Sprigs of fresh holly

Glue the moss onto the log. Because this log is meant to be burned, do not use hot glue. Cover the moss with the frankincense and myrrh potpourri. Glue on the cinnamon sticks, star anise, whole cloves, and pine cones. Drop the related fragrant oils onto the moss and spices. Add a red or green satin bow, a little feathered dove or cardinal (to be removed before burning), and sprigs of fresh holly.

Frankincense and Myrrh Potpourri Recipe

1 quart assorted petals such as marigold blossoms, peony blossoms, rose petals
¼ cup sandalwood chips
1 cup rosemary
2 teaspoons frankincense
1 teaspoon myrrh
1 teaspoon coarsely ground cloves
1 teaspoon crushed Ceylon cinnamon
2 tonka beans, crushed or broken (optional)
1 cup orrisroot
20 drops oils, 10 each cinnamon and frankincense

This project/recipe by Bob Clark appeared in *Herbal Treasures*.

Herb Wrapping

Herbs can be a novel way to dress up a package and a last minute lifesaver. For a simple country look that is also festive, try the following.

Wrap your package in a very plain paper such as butcher paper, a brown paper bag that has been cut open flat, or newsprint endrolls from your local newspaper. (Most newspapers are only too happy to give away remnant rolls too small for them to use. Don't ask to cut a piece though; take the whole roll.)

Choose a pastel or earthy tone ribbon to complement the paper and add a little interest. Strips of netting, raffia or packing twine can also be used instead and provide interest without dominating the overall look.

Now gather a bundle of your favorite herbs and dried flowers; tie the bow around the stems. Herbs that have been dried or have fairly woody stems work best, such as eucalyptus, tansy, coriander, sage, bay, lavender, yarrow, rosemary, and many others.

Herbal Vinegars

Making your own herbal vinegars may not change your life, but it can certainly transform your culinary habits, as they can be used in virtually every aspect of cooking. With different vinegars and combinations of herbs as well as other ingredients, especially spice and fruits, the possible variations are practically limitless.

See list for combinations of herbs. The biggest mistake most people make when creating herbal vinegars is not using enough herbs. Several sprigs may give a whiff of the herb, but to really get an effect, use about 1 cup of loosely packed fresh herb leaves to 2 cups of vinegar. For dried herbs, use ½ cup for 2 cups of vinegar.

Gather fresh herbs by mid-morning after the dew has dried. If the plants are muddy, gently wash and dry them with towels. Carefully strip the leaves from the stems. Place the herbs in a clean, sterilized jar and use a spoon to bruise them slightly. Pour the vinegar over the herbs and cover the jar tightly. Do not heat the vinegar. Let the herb-vinegar mixture steep in a dark place at room temperature. Shake the jar every couple of days and taste the vinegar after a week.

If the flavor is not strong enough, let it stand for another one to three weeks, checking the flavor weekly. If an even stronger flavor is desired, repeat the steeping process with fresh herbs.

When the flavor is right, strain the vinegar, fill the clean, sterilized bottles, cap them tightly, and label them.

Note that commercial mint vinegars are often sweetened with sugar and brightened with garish green food coloring. This is not to my taste, but if you prefer a sweetened mint vinegar, you can add sugar to taste to any of the mint vinegar recipes found here.

HERB VINEGAR COMBINATIONS

Red Wine Vinegars

* Thyme, rosemary, hyssop, fennel, oregano, and garlic
* Basil, rosemary, tarragon, marjoram, mint, bay, dill seed, black peppercorns, whole allspice berries, and cloves
* Lemon thyme, rosemary, and black peppercorns
* Rosemary, savory, sage, basil, bay, and garlic
* Cilantro, sage, rosemary, bay, and hot red pepper
* Mint, rosemary, bay, sage, tarragon, garlic, whole cloves, cinnamon stick, black peppercorns, allspice berries, and mustard seed
* Marjoram, basil, mint, dill, rosemary, bay, whole allspice berries, black peppercorns, and cloves
* Lemongrass, lemon verbena, lemon zest, and green peppercorns
* Cilantro, garlic, and fresh gingerroot
* Marjoram, burnet, and lemon balm

Sherry Vinegars

* Basil, rosemary, tarragon, dill, sorrel, mint, chives, and garlic
* Rosemary, oregano, sage, basil, parsley, garlic, and black peppercorns
* Shallot, thyme, and bay
* Sage, whole allspice berries, cloves, and cinnamon stick

White Wine Vinegars

* Basil, parsley, fennel, and garlic
* Oregano, cilantro, garlic, and hot red pepper
* Mint, lemon balm, and lemon basil
* Rosemary, thyme, marjoram, savory, lavender, bay, garlic, and hot red pepper
* Orange mint, coriander seeds, garlic, and orange zest
* Marjoram, burnet, thyme, tarragon, parsley, and chives
* Parsley, lovage, chervil, savory, thyme, rosemary, tarragon, shallots, and black peppercorns
* Mint and cardamom seeds
* Dill, mint, and garlic cloves
* Borage, dill and shallots
* Tarragon, chervil, borage, watercress, garlic, and hot red pepper
* Savory, tarragon, chervil, basil, and chives

This project appeared in *Herbal Vinegar*, by Maggie Oster.

Fragrant Potpourri Candles

Transform homemade or purchased candles into exquisite, fragrant gifts and decorations. When lit, the heat from this candle will release the oils and fragrance of the potpourri. As it burns down, its light will dramatically silhouette the potpourri pattern. For an attractive candle holder, use an inverted glass goblet, filled with potpourri. Or, simply place the candle on a piece of lace. You will need:

- Candle, at least 2½ inches in diameter and not more than 6 inches high
- Clear spray paint or hair spray
- Paper and scissors
- White glue (such as Designer Tacky Glue)
- Potpourri
- Decorations such as tiny whole flowers (ammobium and acroclinium are nice), spices, tiny pine cones, small bows
- Ice pick (or similar tool)
- Essential oil
- Paraffin, with 143° to 145° F. melting point
- 2 large cans (tall enough to accommodate the candle)
- saucepan
- strong cord
- nylon stocking

Directions

1. Spray the candle with clear spray paint or hair spray to help the glue adhere.
2. Plan your design, using a wreath, tree, or bell for Christmas (or appropriate symbols for other holidays, such as a heart for Valentine's Day). Cut from paper a silhouette of your chosen motif, and attach it to the candle. This makes a kind of reverse stencil — potpourri will adhere everywhere but where the motif is attached.
3. Apply thick, white glue to the candle where you want the potpourri to adhere. Work a section at a

time, pressing the potpourri onto the glued areas. Do not glue potpourri to the top or bottom of the candle. When glue is dry, remove the reverse stencil and glue on the additional decorations, such as small flowers or cones, to outline and ornament the holiday motif. Allow glue to dry for 12 to 24 hours. Shake off excess potpourri.

4. To scent the candle, heat the ice pick and make five holes about 1 inch deep around the wick. Place a couple of drops of essential oil in each hole; the same oil can be added to the molten wax before dipping (see Step 5).

5. Fill a large can of cool tap water and have ready. Melt the paraffin in another large can set in a pan of boiling water. Use only enough water to melt the wax; do not allow the water to overflow. If the wick is short, tightly tie a 6–8-inch piece of strong cord to it. When the wax has totally melted and reached a temperature of 185° to 200° F., you may add a few drops of essential oils.

Place the container of hot wax and the container of cool water next to each other. Pick up the candle by its extended wick and lower it into the molten paraffin for a couple of seconds. Take it out of the hot wax, and immediately lower it into the cool water. Repeat this procedure once or twice. If desired, you can build up a thicker coating by repeated dippings, but the potpourri will not show as well. For taller candles, you may have to dip the bottom half, invert, and then dip the top.

6. Untie the wick extension, and admire! When cooled, polish with an old nylon stocking, if desired.

This project by Bob Clark appeared in *Herbal Treasures*.

Scented Pine-Cone Mix

A bag of scented cones, decorated with Christmas-plaid ribbon makes a thoughtful gift or an attractive bazaar or shop item.

- 6 ounces assorted cones (red pine, spruce, hemlock, tamarack, or other medium- to small-sized cones)
- 2 ounces orange peel, dried (large-cut or cut in long strips)
- 1½ ounces orrisroot, in as large chunks as possible
- 1 ounce cinnamon pieces, 1- to 3-inch
- 1 ounce whole hibiscus flowers (for color, texture, and a weak fixative)
- ½ ounce bay leaves (or lemon eucalyptus)
- 1½ drams Spice Mix Oil: 21 drops each of cinnamon, allspice, and sweet orange or bergamot oils, 15 drops of clove oil, and 12 drops of nutmeg oil

Mix all together and let set, covered, for 3 weeks. Shake often.

Recipe by Sally Booth-Brezina appeared in *Herbal Treasures*.

Balsam Woods Potpourri

This is a very traditional scent for the holidays!

- 3 cups balsam fir tips
- 1 cup rosebuds and petals
- ½ cup lavender blossoms
- ½ cup lemon or orange peel
- ½ cup oakmoss
- 1 teaspoon whole cloves
- 1 teaspoon whole allspice
- 3-inch stick cinnamon, broken
- 2 tablespoons orrisroot
- A few drops of essential oils

Mix all ingredients together. Let cure in a dark place for 4 to 6 weeks, stirring weekly.

Recipe by Wendy J. Newmeyer appeared in *Herbal Treasures*.

Scented Drawer Liners

You will need some wallpaper with an attractive pattern and not too shiny a surface. Use the cheaper wallpapers that are not "wipe-clean" or "steam-resistant" as they tend to absorb the most. Begin by cutting the wallpaper to the size of the drawers that it is to line.

Make up your favorite sweet-bag mixture, see receipe. Put a few drops of a matching essential oil on a cotton ball. Rub the cotton ball on the underside of the wallpaper. Sprinkle the sweet-bag mixture quite thickly over the pattern side of one piece of liner. Lay another on top and sprinkle that with the mixture. Continue until all the liners are used. Roll them up and seal them in a plastic bag. Leave them for 6 weeks.

Brush away all the sweet-bag mixture from the paper before lining your drawers. Reserve the mixture to use as filling for sachets. You can also rub the insides of cupboards and drawers with the predominate sweet oil used on the liners and in the sweet-bag mixture.

OLD COLONIAL SWEET-BAG MIXTURE

- 2 ounces rose petals
- 1 ounce lavender
- 1 ounce hyssop
- 2 tablespoons lime peel, crushed
- 2 tablespoons blade mace, crushed
- 2 drops patchouli oil
- 2 drops vetiver oil

Put the dried rose petals, lavender and hyssop in a large mixing bowl. Add the lime peel and mace and mix with your fingers. Add the oils, 1 drop at a time, and mix after each drop. Put the mixture in a closed container and allow to age for 6 weeks, shaking every other day.

This project appeared in *Natural Fragrances*, by Gail Duff.

MINT NUT BREAD

2½ cups flour
1 cup firmly packed brown sugar
3½ teaspoons baking powder
3 tablespoons oil
1½ cups milk or ¾ cup apple juice and ¾ cup milk
1 egg
1 cup chopped walnuts
1 cup chopped fresh mint (⅓ scant cup, dried)

Preheat oven to 350° F. Mix the flour, sugar, and baking powder in a large mixing bowl. Whisk together the oil, milk, and egg. Blend the mixtures together. Add the walnuts and mint.

Bake in greased bread pans in the preheated oven for 50 to 60 minutes. Cool and slice. Ages and freezes well.

Recipe by Ronda Schooley Bretz appeared in *Herbal Treasures*.

MARGARET'S TURKEY-HERB BASTE

For a nice gift, package the dry ingredients prettily and tie on a tag with instructions to mix with ½ cup white wine and 2 tablespoons lemon juice.

¼ teaspoon dry mustard
¼ teaspoon nutmeg
¼ teaspoon allspice
2 teaspoons dried parsley
1 teaspoon sage
1 teaspoon fennel seed

1 teaspoon salt (optional)
1 teaspoon pepper
½ cup white wine (such as Chablis)
2 tablespoons lemon juice

Using a mortar and pestle, grind all the herbs and spices together. Add to the wine and lemon juice, and blend together. Before baking, brush the inside and rub the outside of the turkey with the mixture. Stuff with your favorite dressing. Use remaining mixture to baste the turkey as it cooks.

Recipe by Mrs. Margaret J. Springer appeared in *Herbal Treasures*.

GINGER LIQUEUR

*This easy-to-make liqueur
will put a little zip in your holiday treats.*

½ cup crystallized ginger
2 cups vodka
½ cup sugar syrup

Add all ingredients together. Steep for 2 weeks in a quart jar. Strain and it is ready to serve. This liqueur has a real zing to it and will be enjoyed by a true ginger lover. Makes a unique addition to meat and poultry marinades.

YIELD: 2 PINT PLUS.

This recipe appeared in *Country Fresh Gifts*, collected from Storey's Country Wisdom Bulletins.

HARDWAYE HERB MUSTARD

Homemade mustards packed in small jars you have decorated with a ribbon or a calico jar cover make a festive addition to any table. This mustard thickens better if you use whole wheat flour. You may substitute white wine for part of the vinegar. If you have fresh herbs, use double the amount. This mustard will keep in the refrigerator for several months.

4 cups vinegar
2 cups dry mustard
2 cups unbleached or whole wheat flour
1¼ cups sugar
1 clove garlic, crushed or pressed
¼ cup mixed dried herbs, such as basil, thyme, parsley, marjoram, and rosemary

Combine mustard, flour and sugar in a bowl. Add the vinegar to the dry mixture, stirring well until lump-free. A whisk may help here. Stir in the garlic and herbs. Let the mixture stand overnight, then stir again. If the mustard is too thin, add more flour. Pour into covered crocks or jars.

Recipe by Betsy Williams appeared in *Herbal Treasures*.

RELATED TITLES OF INTEREST FROM STOREY COMMUNICATIONS, INC.

Christmas Trees: Growing and Selling Trees, Wreaths, and Greens by Lewis Hill. Hill covers it all: selecting and preparing a site; cultivation and maintenance; managing production and harvest; finding wholesale and retail markets, a grower's calendar; and associations. 160 pages $9.95 #566-9

A Gift Book of Herbs and Herbal Flowers edited by Rosemary Hemphill. This beautifully illustrated, slipcase-covered book includes a potpourri of herb and flower prose, poems, recipes, crafts, and folklore, representing 32 different herbs and flowers. Full-color illustrations and photographs with printed endpapers. 112 pages $14.00 #885-4

Herbal Treasures, Inspiring Month-by-Month Projects for Gardening, Cooking, and Crafts by Phyllis V. Shaudys. A compendium of the best herb crafts, recipes, and gardening ideas. Gardeners, cooks, and crafts people alike will find a vast array of projects and recipes to try. 320 pages $16.95 #618-5

Herbs for the Holidays, A Treasury of Decorations by Sal Gilbertie. Learn how to make gloriously fragrant herb creations to beautify your home for the holidays. Thirty different projects using low-cost or free natural materials. Complete instructions and lovely color photographs. 128 pages $21.95 (hardcover) #871-4

Herbs for Weddings & Other Celebrations, a Treasury of Recipes, Gifts & Decorations by Bertha Reppert. Lovely designs for everything from bouquets to wreaths and cake decorations, plus tips on preserving flowers and herbs for years to come. Includes step-by-step instructions, color photographs and 75 recipes. 200 pages $16.95 (paperback) #864-1; $24.95 (hardcover) #866-8

The Herbal Body Book, A Natural Approach to Healthier Hair, Skin, and Nails by Stephanie Tourles. How to transform common herbs, fruits, and grains into safe, economical, and natural personal care items. Contains over 100 recipes to make facial scrubs, hair rinses, shampoos, soaps, cleansing lotions, moisturizers, lip balms, toothpaste, powders, insect repellants, and more! 128 pages $12.95 #880-3

STOREY COMMUNICATIONS, INC.
1-800-441-5700 • 8:30 am to 10:00 pm • 7 Days a Week
For ordering information, please see the back cover.